Hello, America!

Gateway Arch

by Kaitlyn Duling

Bullfrog
Books

Ideas for Parents and Teachers

Bullfrog Books let children practice reading informational text at the earliest reading levels. Repetition, familiar words, and photo labels support early readers.

Before Reading

- Discuss the cover photo. What does it tell them?
- Look at the picture glossary together. Read and discuss the words.

Read the Book

- "Walk" through the book and look at the photos. Let the child ask questions. Point out the photo labels.
- Read the book to the child, or have him or her read independently.

After Reading

- Prompt the child to think more. Ask: Have you seen the Gateway Arch, either in person or in a picture? How would you describe it?

Bullfrog Books are published by Jump!
5357 Penn Avenue South
Minneapolis, MN 55419
www.jumplibrary.com

Library of Congress Cataloging-in-Publication Data

Names: Duling, Kaitlyn.
Title: Gateway Arch / by Kaitlyn Duling.
Description: Jump!, Inc. : Minneapolis, Minnesota, 2018.
Series: Hello, America!
"Bullfrog Books." Includes index.
Audience: K-3. | Audience: Ages 5-8.
Identifiers: LCCN 2017027409 (print)
LCCN 2017027729 (ebook)
ISBN 9781624966583 (e-book)
ISBN 9781620318645 (hard cover: alk. paper)
Subjects: LCSH: Gateway Arch (Saint Louis, Mo.)
Juvenile literature. | Saint Louis (Mo.)—Buildings, structures, etc.—Juvenile literature.
Classification: LCC F474.S265 (ebook) | LCC F474.
S265 G3724 2018 (print) | DDC 977.8/66—dc23
LC record available at https://lccn.loc.gov/2017027409

Editor: Kirsten Chang
Book Designer: Molly Ballanger
Photo Researcher: Molly Ballanger

Photo Credits: SNEHIT/Shutterstock, cover; saraporn/Shutterstock, 1, 22; SunChan/iStock, 3; stevegeer/iStock, 4, 23tl; Davel5957/iStock, 5, 23tr; planet5D LLC/Shutterstock, 6; Bettmann/Getty, 7; Andy Magee/Shutterstock, 8–9, 23bl; Historic Map Works LLC/Getty, 10–11; GREG RYAN/Alamy, 12; Fotosearch/Stringer/Getty, 13; joe daniel price/Getty, 14–15, 23mr; f11photo/Shutterstock, 16–17, 20–21 (background); Kelly/Mooney Photography/Getty, 18; digidreamgrafix/iStock, 18–19; Dragon Images/Shutterstock, 20–21 (foreground); Imagine CG Images/Shutterstock, 23ml; DVARG/Shutterstock, 23br; Andrey _ KZ/iStock, 24.

Printed in the United States of America at Corporate Graphics in North Mankato, Minnesota.

Table of Contents

Go West

Look up!
It's the
Gateway Arch.

It is in St. Louis, Missouri.

Gateway Arch

St. Louis, Missouri

5

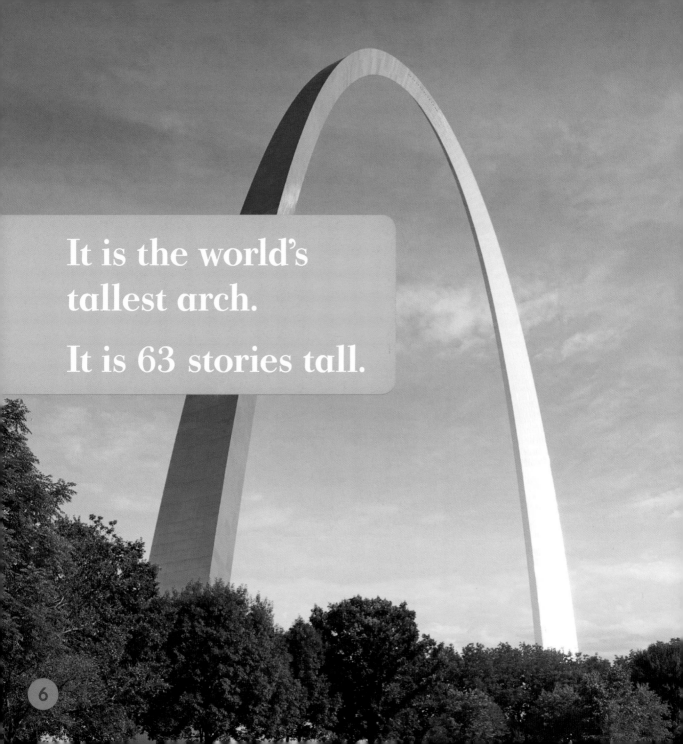

It is the world's tallest arch.

It is 63 stories tall.

It was built in 1965.

What is it made of?

Steel.

It shines!

New
York City,
1800s

Why was it built?

Many years ago, the country was small. Most people lived in the East.

11

But some moved west.

The country grew.

People stopped in St. Louis before going west.

St. Louis, 1800s

The arch is a symbol of the city.

It is the gateway to the West.

Today, many people visit.
We can go up.
We ride a tram.

Look out!

We see the city.

We had fun at the
Gateway Arch!

21

The Arch Up Close

steel
The arch is made up of 142 stainless steel sections.

windows
The 32 windows at the top are 7 inches (18 centimeters) by 27 inches (69 centimeters).

leg width
The legs are 54 feet (16 meters) wide at the base. They get smaller near the top.

arch width
The legs of the arch are 630 feet (192 meters) apart at the base.

Picture Glossary

arch
A structure with straight sides and a curved top.

St. Louis
A large city in the state of Missouri.

gateway
A passage into or out of a place.

symbol
An object that represents something else.

steel
A hard, strong material made by heating iron and mixing it with carbon.

tram
A car that moves on cables, like an elevator.

Index

To Learn More

Learning more is as easy as 1, 2, 3.

1) Go to www.factsurfer.com

2) Enter "GatewayArch" into the search box.

3) Click the "Surf" button to see a list of websites.

With factsurfer.com, finding more information is just a click away.